CARYL CHURCHILL

Caryl Churchill has written fo[r] [sta]g[e,] [tele]vision
and radio. Her stage plays include *Owners* (Royal Court
Theatre Upstairs, 1972); *Objections to Sex and Violence*
(Royal Court, 1975); *Light Shining in Buckinghamshire*
(Joint Stock on tour incl. Theatre Upstairs, 1976);
Vinegar Tom (Monstrous Regiment on tour, incl. Half
Moon and ICA, 1976); *Traps* (Theatre Upstairs, 1977),
Cloud Nine (Joint Stock on tour incl. Royal Court,
London, 1979, then Theatre de Lys, New York, 1981);
Three More Sleepless Nights (Soho Poly and Theatre
Upstairs, 1980); *Top Girls* (Royal Court, London, then
Public Theatre, New York, 1982); *Fen* (Joint Stock on
tour, incl. Almeida and Royal Court, London, then
Public Theatre, New York, 1983); *Softcops* (RSC at the
Pit, 1984); *A Mouthful of Birds* with David Lan (Joint
Stock on tour, incl. Royal Court, 1986); *Serious Money*
(Royal Court and Wyndham's, London, then Public
Theatre, New York, 1987); *Icecream* (Royal Court, 1989);
Mad Forest (Central School of Speech and Drama, then
Royal Court, 1990, then New York Theatre Workshop,
1991); *Lives of the Great Poisoners* with Orlando Gough
and Ian Spink (Second Stride on tour, incl. Riverside
Studios, London, 1991); *The Skriker* (Royal National
Theatre, 1994; Public Theatre, New York, 1996);
Thyestes translated from Seneca (Royal Court Theatre
Upstairs, 1994); *Hotel* with Orlando Gough and Ian
Spink (Second Stride on tour, incl. The Place, London,
1997); *This is a Chair* (London International Festival of
Theatre at the Royal Court, 1997); *Blue Heart* (Out of
Joint on tour, incl. Royal Court Theatre, 1997).

Other works by this author in the same series

Light Shining in Buckinghamshire
Traps
Cloud Nine
Icecream
Mad Forest
The Skriker
Thyestes (translated from Seneca)
Blue Heart

Collections

Shorts
    Lovesick
    Abortive
    Not Not Not Not Not Enough Oxygen
    Schreber's Nervous Illness
    The Hospital at the Time of the Revolution
    The Judge's Wife
    The After-Dinner Joke
    Seagulls
    Three More Sleepless Nights
    Hot Fudge

Plays: Three
    A Mouthful of Birds (co-author: David Lan)
    Icecream
    Mad Forest
    Lives of the Great Poisoners
      (co-authors: Orlando Gough and Ian Spink)
    The Skriker
    Thyestes (translated from Seneca)

CARYL CHURCHILL

This is a Chair

THEATRE
COMMUNICATIONS
GROUP
NEW YORK

A Nick Hern Book

This is a Chair is published by Theatre Communications Group, Inc., 355 Lexington Avenue, New York, NY 10017, by special arrangement with Nick Hern Books Limited

Cover design from Magritte's *The Treachery of Images*, Los Angeles County Museum of Art, USA

CIP catalog information for this book is available from the Library of Congress

ISBN 978 1 55936 177 4

This is a Chair was first performed at the Royal Court Theatre at the Duke of York's, London, on 25 June 1997, with the following cast:

JULIAN	Linus Roache
MARY	Amanda Plummer
FATHER	Sam Kelly
MOTHER	Marion Bailey
MURIEL	Harriet Spencer
TED	Euan Bremner
ANN	Diane Parish
JOHN	Lennie James
DEIRDRE	Liz Smith
POLLY	Helena McCarthy
TOM	Desmond Barrit
LEO	Timothy Spall
CHARLIE	Andy Serkis
MADDY	Cecelia Noble
ERIC	Ray Winstone

Directed by Stephen Daldry
Designed by Ian MacNeil
Lighting by Lizz Poulter

Characters

JULIAN
MARY

FATHER
MOTHER
MURIEL

TED
ANN
JOHN

DEIRDRE
POLLY

TOM
LEO
CHARLIE

ERIC
MADDY

**The title of each scene must be clearly
displayed or announced.**

The War in Bosnia

JULIAN *is waiting in a London street holding a bunch of flowers.*

MARY *arrives.*

MARY
I'm so sorry.

JULIAN
That's all right, don't worry.

MARY
Have you been here ages?

JULIAN
I got you these.

MARY
They're beautiful.

JULIAN
I don't know what you like.

MARY
Thank you very much.

JULIAN
I like orange and blue together, I don't know if you do, I thought of roses but I think roses are a bit dull,

I don't like pink and red very much as colours, I don't mind yellow but I thought these.

MARY
Listen, I'm afraid there's a problem.

JULIAN
Yes.

MARY
I've made a stupid mistake.

JULIAN
Never mind.

MARY
No but I've made two different arrangements for the same evening, I've doublebooked myself, I don't know how I can be so stupid.

JULIAN
So you have to make a phonecall or . . . ?

MARY
No, it's really awful, what I have to do is jump in a cab and go whizzing off. Because I have to be there by halfpast seven.

JULIAN
Something starts at halfpast seven?

MARY
Yes and I couldn't reach the other person and anyway the tickets and . . .

JULIAN
Don't worry.

MARY
It is a concert I particularly . . .

JULIAN
Yes of course. We'd better look for a cab.

MARY
It was the arrangement I made first you see and
somehow it slipped my mind and I thought we
might have time for a drink anyway but then I was
late finishing work and there was a holdup on the
tube it stopped in the tunnel for about five minutes
people were starting to get nervous you could see
from the way they kept on reading or just staring into
space but deliberately because they were getting
nervous and anyway can we make it another time
I'm really sorry.

JULIAN
Don't worry.

MARY
What about Tuesday?

JULIAN
I can't do Tuesdays.

MARY
Or Thursday, no wait I can't do Thursday, Friday oh
shit, the week after, any night you like, not
Wednesday.

JULIAN
Thursday then.

MARY
Thursday week then.

JULIAN
Same time same place?

MARY
Yes this is good for me. I wont be late.

JULIAN
Don't worry. There's a cab.

MARY
I'm really sorry.

JULIAN
Byebye.

Pornography and Censorship

FATHER, MOTHER *and* MURIEL *at dinner.*

FATHER
Is Muriel going to eat her dinner?

MOTHER
Yes, eat up, Muriel.

FATHER
Have a special bite of daddy's.

MOTHER
Yes, eat up, Muriel.

FATHER
Muriel, if you don't eat your dinner you know what's going to happen to you.

MOTHER
Yes, eat up, Muriel.

The Labour Party's Slide to the Right

TED *and* ANN *in Ann and her boy-friend's third-floor flat.*

TED
I don't believe it.

ANN
You did that.

TED
John, John get in here quick.

ANN
You did that coming in here.

JOHN *comes in.*

JOHN
I can't find nothing in the bedroom.

TED
John you won't believe this.

JOHN
Where is he?

ANN
It's your fault coming in here.

TED
He ran on the balcony and jumped over.

JOHN
He what?

TED
I can't look.

ANN
I'm going down. You did it, I'll tell everyone you did
it, why can't you keep out of my life.

ANN *goes*.

TED
I just said we've had enough of you. I didn't touch
him.

JOHN
He knew what we was here for.

TED
He knew we were here to say you got our sister on
drugs.

JOHN
And we said that.

TED
That's all we said.

JOHN
We weren't going to kill him or nothing.

TED
We were going to give him a smack.

JOHN
That's all right. Anyone expects a smack.

TED
We'll say exactly what happened. We don't need a
story, do we, I mean what happened is what happened
is perfectly all right.

JOHN
He might not be dead you know.

TED
I can't look.

JOHN
I'll look.

TED
Go on then.

JOHN
Yes I'm going to.

TED
He must have been out of his head is what it is.

JOHN
They'll see what he was on at the hospital.

TED
Maybe it's something he was going to do whether we
come or not.

JOHN
Don't be stupid.

TED
So are you going to look or what?

JOHN
Yes I'm going to look.

TED
What a stupid bastard.

JOHN
Do you think she's down there by now? I'll have a
look.

Animal Conservation and Third World Economics: the Ivory Trade

DEIRDRE *and* POLLY.

DEIRDRE
I'm going to hospital on Monday.

POLLY
Nothing serious?

DEIRDRE
No not at all but I've got to swallow a tube.

POLLY
I could go with you if you like.

DEIRDRE
No, it's nothing, I've done it before. You can do it with drugs or without.

POLLY
With.

DEIRDRE
I did do with the first time, I wasn't given a choice, but last time they said it only takes a couple of minutes do you want to try without. I said how often do people do that and they said about fifty fifty and I said and what do they say about it afterwards and they said oh they're fine about it, honestly, but of course if

you haven't anything to do this afternoon and don't
mind being drugged up - so put like that of course it
was a challenge.

POLLY
And was it horrible?

DEIRDRE
The worst bit's when it goes over the throat. You have
to keep breathing deeply, like being in labour except
not. But everything taking second place to your body.
And when it's over you feel terrific. I walked home
because I'd got a whole extra afternoon but that was
stupid because I got exhausted because I hadn't eaten
or drunk anything since half past seven. And of course
at the time I thought it was good not putting poison in
my body but afterwards I thought they were just trying
to save money.

POLLY
Of course they were. Didn't you realise that?

DEIRDRE
So maybe on Monday I'll have the drugs.

POLLY
I'd definitely have the drugs.

DEIRDRE
I probably will. Yes I think I'll definitely go for the
drugs.

Hong Kong

TOM *and* LEO.

TOM
How could you do that you lied to me yes no I don't
want to hear

LEO
very funny I don't care I don't care what you

TOM
just about enough

LEO
and I suppose you never?

TOM
why don't we just why don't we just now wait a minute

LEO
can't stand it can't

TOM
get this sorted out. Why in particular?

LEO
no good coming in now and saying

TOM
but listen why don't we just

LEO
too late

TOM
impossible to talk to

LEO
should have thought of that

TOM
you are so

LEO
piss off.

TOM
Not the first time

LEO
can't trust you with the simplest

TOM
no point in even

LEO
for instance and then last week you

TOM
how could you do that

LEO
and what you said was you wouldn't dream

TOM
and it doesn't even stand up I'd have to be stupid

LEO
stupid stupid stupid

TOM
break your neck

LEO
and you smell bad

TOM
if you could see yourself

LEO
piggy eyes piggy eyes piggy eyes

TOM
don't just don't even start don't just I'm warning you
now don't

LEO
never did anyway

TOM
what the fuck you

LEO
on Wednesday at halfpast eleven when we'd specifically

TOM
two hundred pounds I don't understand how you can

LEO
because that's where you were don't bother denying it

TOM
and then you blame me

LEO
because I saw her in Safeways and she

TOM
don't let me see him again that's all or I'll

LEO
in our own bed

TOM
no.

LEO
I'm going to

TOM
fine by me

LEO
because I never

TOM
don't fancy you any more have to imagine

LEO
every time you come into the house my heart

TOM
haven't ever liked you

LEO
disgust me.

Their friend CHARLIE *arrives.*

TOM
well well well well well

LEO
long time

TOM
wet coat

CHARLIE
ah lovely

TOM
how you

CHARLIE
traffic

TOM
pretty busy

CHARLIE
seen old Joey lately because I've

LEO
house in the south of France

CHARLIE
running all over town trying to

TOM
rollmop herrings

CHARLIE
must have been terrible for you

LEO
and you've heard about Rose and

TOM
so we put in an offer of twenty thousand less than

CHARLIE
halfway to America by now.

LEO
So how's Wendy are you still

CHARLIE
terrible headaches

TOM
always remember that summer when

CHARLIE
the train to Brindisi

LEO
and the smell of the rain on the dust

CHARLIE
I do of course understand her point of view I wouldn't
want to

TOM
always was a bit

LEO
emphasis on personal development

CHARLIE
her mother screeching positively screeching I couldn't

TOM
a good acupuncturist

LEO
up at halfpast five in the summer when the light

CHARLIE
my cousin in Australia

TOM
on the other hand

LEO
yes I wouldn't want to

CHARLIE
helps to talk things over with

TOM
not getting any younger

CHARLIE
don't know what to think

LEO
and is it this weekend we put the clocks back or is it
back I never I have to work it out on my fingers same
with America if I

TOM
stay to supper?

CHARLIE
my aunt's cat it got hit by a car and I said I'd

LEO
onion soup

CHARLIE
you are the loveliest

LEO
if you want to go to a movie, I haven't seen

TOM
supposed to be terrifying

CHARLIE
though I didn't think so much of his

LEO
the bit where they fell down the stairs and the

CHARLIE
so I'll call you next week and maybe we can

LEO
that would be lovely

TOM
great to see you

LEO
give my love to

CHARLIE
sorry I'm a bit

LEO
next week.

CHARLIE *goes.*

LEO
putting on weight

TOM
having rather a difficult

LEO
work's not what it was of course but he didn't

TOM
why don't we just get a curry in I really fancy a

LEO
so tired I could

TOM
hot bath

LEO
hey

TOM
yes well

LEO
exhausted

TOM
quarrelling is so

LEO
oh god

TOM
come here and let me

LEO
you don't really

TOM
let me just

LEO
because I do still

TOM
you're such a

LEO
not all my

TOM
don't start

LEO
love it when you

The Northern Ireland Peace Process

FATHER, MOTHER *and* MURIEL *at dinner.*

FATHER
Is Muriel going to eat her dinner?

MOTHER
Yes, eat up, Muriel.

FATHER
Have a special bite of daddy's.

MOTHER
Yes, eat up, Muriel.

FATHER
Muriel, if you don't eat your dinner you know what's going to happen to you.

MOTHER
Yes, eat up, Muriel.

Genetic Engineering

ERIC *and* MADDY *on their way to bed.*

MADDY
What was that? was that a bomb but far more likely

ERIC
no far more likely

MADDY
more likely a building some kind of construction

ERIC
demolition

MADDY
some kind of building

ERIC
some kind of building site or a road accident a crash
but it's the wrong kind of sound for that it was more

MADDY
what, more

ERIC
more whoosh in it not so much metal

MADDY
like a firework can be like that like a rocket

ERIC
yes but no it was bigger

MADDY
no but they can those public ones set off huge

ERIC
so anyway I don't think it was a bomb anyway

MADDY
no I never thought it was a bomb. We could notice
what time it is just to

ERIC
yes because you remember that time

MADDY
yes we said what was that but we didn't think anything
of it

ERIC
no I did think

MADDY
and later it had been ten past one and we said

ERIC
yes you said that must be what we heard because we'd
just sat down to the soup

MADDY
yes we said we must have heard it because it was ten
past one.

ERIC
Well it's near enough half past eleven.

MADDY
I'm going to bed.

ERIC
Go on then, I'm coming.

MADDY
Yes but do come. You'll sit.

ERIC
No I am coming.

MADDY
I'm not sure I'm sleepy anyway.

ERIC
I'm not going to have a bath I had a bath yesterday
I don't feel like a bath.

MADDY
No don't have a bath have one in the morning.

The Impact of Capitalism on the Former Soviet Union

End.